**Genre** Fantasy

MW00571689

 Essential Question
How can we classify and
categorize things?

Dog Bones

by Nora Carson
illustrated by Betsy Day

Chapter 1
Why Is Max Excited?

This is Max. He has saved a lot of bones. He is proud of his collection.

One day, Max learns about a contest. The contest is for the biggest bone. He thinks he can win.

Chapter 2
Where Are the Bones?

Max needs to dig up all of his bones. Where did he bury them? He sniffs and sniffs and sniffs.

4

Max starts to dig. He finds a round ball, but no bones. Where did he bury them?

Max walks to another spot and digs. Now he finds a whole bunch of bones. There are so many! How will he find the biggest one?

6

Max starts to sort the bones.

"These are small," says Max.
"I will put them in a pile."

7

Chapter 3
What Does Max Find?

Max digs up four more bones.

He says, "These bones are bigger.
I will make a new pile."

He digs again and finds only one more. It is the one he was looking for.

"This bone is the biggest," he says.

Now he is ready to go to the contest.

On the way, Max sees his
friend Bob.

Bob says, "I had trouble finding
bones. I have none."

"Come with me," says Max. "This
bone is large enough for two. We
will enter the contest together."

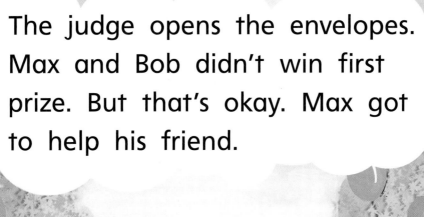

The judge opens the envelopes. Max and Bob didn't win first prize. But that's okay. Max got to help his friend.

Respond to Reading

Retell

Use your own words to retell *Dog Bones.*

Character	Clue	Point of View

Text Evidence

1. Look at page 2. How does Max feel about his collection of bones? Point of View

2. Look at page 10. How does Bob feel? Point of View

3. How can you tell that *Dog Bones* is a fantasy? Genre

Compare Texts
How do we sort things?

Sorting Balls

How can we sort balls? Let's sort them by size! These balls are small.

These balls are bigger.

This ball is the biggest.

 Make Connections
Look at both selections. What did you learn about sorting? Text to Text

Focus on Genre

Fantasy A fantasy is a story with made-up characters, settings, and actions. A fantasy could not happen in real life.

What to Look for In *Dog Bones,* the animals talk, read, and enter a contest. Real animals don't talk, read, or enter contests.

Your Turn

Write your own idea for a fantasy about an animal. What kind of animal is it? What does the animal do?